SAQUON BARKLEY

Marylou Morano Kjelle

PUBLISHERS

2001 SW 31st Avenue
Hallandale, FL 33009

www.mitchelllane.com

First Edition, 2020.
Author: Marylou Morano Kjelle
Designer: Ed Morgan
Editor: Lisa Petrillo

Series: Blue Banner Biographies
Title: Saquon Barkley / by Marylou Morano Kjelle

Hallandale, FL : Mitchell Lane Publishers, [2020]

Library bound ISBN: 9781680204995
eBook ISBN: 9781680205008

Contents

CHAPTER ONE

Drafted!

SAQUON **BARKLEY** always knew that one day he would play football for the National Football League (NFL). When he was three years old, he and his dad, Alibay, would watch the New York Jets games on television. Saquon's favorite Jets player was No. 28, running back, Curtis Martin.

"When I grow up, I'm going to be No. 28," he would tell his father.

Fast forward 18 years. The date is April 26, 2018, and the place is the AT&T Stadium in Arlington, Texas. The event is the 83rd annual NFL draft. Barkley, now a running back for Pennsylvania State University, sits with his family in an off-stage area set up for the draftees. In the sports world, a draft is a common way for a team to choose new players. Late in 2017, Barkley had announced on social media that he would skip his senior year of college and declare himself eligible for the NFL draft.

"God has blessed me with the opportunity to pursue the dream I have had as a little kid of playing in the NFL," Barkley wrote on his Instagram account. "After lots of thought, prayer, and conversation with those closest to me, I have decided to enter the NFL draft."

Barkley was all smiles after learning he was the second overall pick by the New York Giants in the first round of the 2018 NFL draft.

Barkley had broken many records at Penn State, a college famous for its football program. And he was on his way to becoming a college football legend. Some NFL recruiters thought he would be one of the first—if not *the* first—college football player drafted in 2018. But the first team to choose, the Cleveland Browns, selected Baker Mayfield, a quarterback from the University of Oklahoma.

The second pick was about to be announced. Each team had 10 minutes to select its player. Each draftee had his own phone, so that a team could contact him directly with an offer.

Barkley's phone rang. It was Pat Shurmur, head coach of the New York Giants. The Giants wanted to draft Barkley, and he accepted the offer.

"This is the first of many great days as a Giant," Coach Shurmur told him.

"I promise you guys, I won't let you guys down," Barkley replied.

A few seconds later, NFL Commissioner, Roger Goodell's words rang throughout AT&T Stadium loudspeakers:

"With the second pick in the 2018 NFL draft, the New York Giants pick Saquon Barkley, running back from Penn State."

As Giants fans cheered wildly, Barkley placed a Giants cap on his head and headed onstage. There Commissioner Goodell handed him a Giants rookie jersey with his last name and the number "1," indicating he was the Giants' first pick in the 2018 draft.

"I am truly excited for the honor to be part of the New York Giants. That team is about winning and hopefully I can help as soon as possible," Barkley told a sportswriter later that evening. His childhood dream of playing for the NFL had come true. Saquon Barkley had been drafted into the pros!

NFL Commissioner Roger Goodell presented Barkley with a Giants rookie jersey after announcing that he had been drafted by the New York team.

"Little Barry Sanders"

BARKLEY **WAS** **BORN** in the Bronx, New York, a borough of New York City, on February 7, 1997. His mother, Tonya Johnson, works in retail customer service and part time in a tax office. Saquon's father, Alibay Barkley, is a cook and former amateur boxer. Saquon has an older half-brother, Rashad, an older sister, Shaqouna, and younger twin siblings, a brother Ali, and a sister Aliyah.

Alibay also wanted to be a boxing champion. He was inspired by his uncle, Iran Barkley, a three-time World Boxing Council middleweight champion. Alibay grew up in a dangerous part of the Bronx full of crime and drugs. He battled a drug addiction, and was arrested several times. When he was 19 years old, Alibay spent a year in prison on a gun possession charge.

"I was a good boxer, but I made bad choices," Alibay later explained to a reporter.

Tonya's relatives lived in Bethlehem Pennsylvania, in a rural area once known for its steel industry. She often visited with Saquon and his sister. Saquon suffered from asthma, and Tonya noticed he breathed better when he was away from the city. When Saquon was 5 years old, his family moved to the Lehigh Valley area of Pennsylvania. At first they lived in Allentown, and then they settled in Coplay, about 6 miles away.

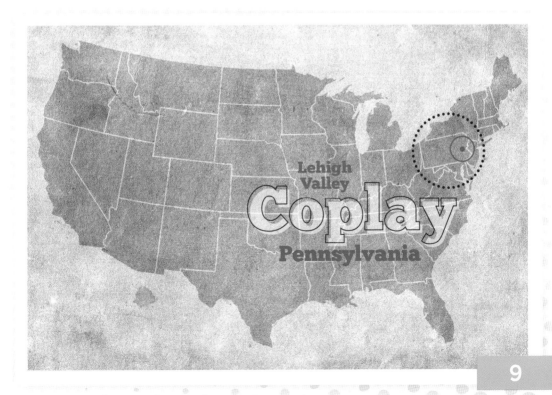

To keep Saquon from making his own bad choices, Alibay tried to get him interested in boxing. But football was Saquon's passion. He joined the nearby youth football team, and when he was 8 years old, Saquon was already showing his talent by running 99-yard touchdowns. People called him "Little Barry Sanders." because his moves on the football field reminded them of football great Barry Sanders. Sanders played running back for the Detroit Lions and is in the football Hall of Fame.

When he was a young boy, Saquon's skill on the football field reminded people of Barry Sanders, the Hall of Famer running back for the Detroit Lions.

"Little Barry Sanders"

When Saquon entered his freshman year at Whitehall High School, he lost confidence in his football ability. He even thought of quitting the Whitehall Zephyrs because he didn't think he was good enough for the team. "I'd tell him, 'You are the fastest and the strongest, but there are things you're going to need to overcome mentally,'" recalled his high school coach Dennis McWhite to a *Sports Illustrated* reporter. Saquon's father also warned him not to quit. "If you quit this, it will be easy to quit jobs, quit relationships, quit on your kids," his dad told him. Saquon's self-confidence returned in his sophomore year, but he struggled with his schoolwork. He only played varsity football part time. The summer before his junior year, while attending a football camp, Saquon met Rutgers University football coach, Kyle Flood. Coach Flood offered Saquon a scholarship to Rutgers in New Jersey, and a chance to play for the Scarlet Knights.

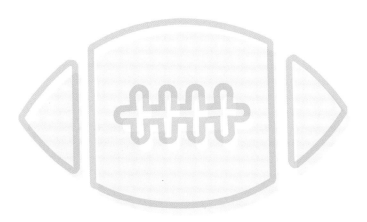

"I remember trying to look so serious and professional, but biting down and smiling," Saquon told a *Sports Illustrated* reporter. "I was like, 'No way this is happening.'" Saquon committed to Rutgers in 2013 when he was still a high school junior. His life changed being offered a scholarship to Rutgers, a famous public university with roots dating back to the 1700s. His confidence increased, his grades rose, and his workouts became more productive. "Rutgers was the turning point for him," recalled his school counselor Linda MacGill. By the time Saquon graduated school, he was ranked the 13th best running back in the country. Saquon was also named "Mr. PA Football-2014," an award given each year to the most skilled high school football players in Pennsylvania.

As Saquon neared graduation, he began to have doubts about attending Rutgers. James Franklin, the head football coach at Penn State University, actively recruited Saquon to attend Penn State and play for the Nittany Lions. Both Penn State and Rutgers are part of a group of 14 colleges that belong to an athletic conference called the Big Ten. It was a difficult decision for Saquon. In the end, Saquon cancelled his scholarship with Rutgers and accepted a scholarship from Penn State.

"It was one of the hardest things I had to do, because I felt like I was going against my word. But I felt like Penn State presented more opportunities for me for the rest of my life,"

"Little Barry Sanders"

As he rushes, Barkley is chased by Buffalo Bulls defenders at a Lions home game on September 12, 2015. During the game, he rushed 115 yards and scored a touchdown, which helped Penn State defeat Buffalo, 27-14.

Saquon told Mark Wogenrich, "I'm forever thankful for Rutgers, Coach Flood and that coaching staff for taking a chance on me," Saquon told a reporter.

Coach Franklin had a good reason to recruit Saquon. Saquon was an awesome running back, and Coach wanted him to play for a college in Pennsylvania, the state where he grew up. "There's something special about playing for your school and your state—kind of being a hometown hero, a local kid who's done well," he told a reporter.

As a freshman at Penn State, Saquon studied broadcast journalism, put on a No. 26 jersey, and played football for the Nittany Lions.

Hear the Lion Roar

BARKLEY **HAD** **MADE** a name for himself at Whitehall High School. By the time he graduated, he had rushed for a total of 3,646 yards and made 63 touchdowns. In his senior year alone, he rushed 1,856 yards and made 31 touchdowns. At the time he entered Penn State, Barkley ranked as the 7th best high school player in Pennsylvania, and he was named first-team All-State. On a national level, he ranked as the 21st best running back, according to 247sports.com.

The unstoppable Saquon Barkley flies over Buffalo Bulls Ryan Williamson (# 26) and Nick Gilbo (# 43) during a long gain at a game at home in Pennsylvania on September 12, 2015.

The position Barkley plays, the running back, is an offensive position. Running backs receive the ball from the quarterback, run—or rush—with the ball, receive the ball when other players pass it, and block opposing team members who are trying to get the ball.

Coaches usually have freshman players sit on the sidelines for the first few games of a season. But Coach Franklin liked the way Barkley played in pre-season practices. He had him play in Penn State's first game of the 2015-16 season against Temple University. Before the game, Barkley told a reporter. "Hopefully, God willing, if I stay healthy, keep my head on straight and keep focused, I can get some playing time [for Penn State] and start a new chapter in my life."

Barkley roared through his three seasons as a Nittany Lion. In his first year, Saquon rushed for 1,076 yards and scored seven touchdowns. As a sophomore, he led the Big Ten with 18 touchdowns, and 1,666 all-purpose yards. He also placed second in rushing yards, with 1,302. That year, Penn State won the Big Ten Football Championship and took the 2016 Big Ten title. In his junior year, Barkley's season rushing total was 1,271 yards, and he scored 18 touchdowns. "All this success that's happened so quickly for him, he's handled it better probably than any young player I've ever been around. I think that's one of the reasons we've had the success we've had," Coach Franklin told a reporter for the Allentown newspaper.

Barkley had been an outstanding player during his first three seasons at Penn State. But many sports commentators believe it was the 2017 Rose Bowl against University of Southern California (USC) where Barkley showed his NFL potential. The Rose Bowl is an annual post-season college football game. It is usually played on New Year's Day at the Rose Bowl Stadium in Pasadena, California. Although the Nittany Lions lost to the USC Trojans 52-49, Barkley impressed fans by making two touchdowns and rushing for 194 yards.

Hear the Lion Roar

Barkley dives with the football as he is tackled by defensive back Taylor Rapp of the Washington Huskies at the Playstation Fiesta Bowl on December 30, 2017.

On December 31, 2017, the Nittany Lions played against the Washington Huskies at the 2017 Fiesta Bowl. Once again, Barkley scored two touchdowns. He also rushed for 137 yards, This time his strong showing on the field helped his team win, 35-28.

Barkley finished his career as a Nittany Lion with 5,538 all-purpose (scrimmage) yards and more than 50 touchdowns. He made more touchdowns than any other player at Penn State. In his three seasons with Penn State, he scored a total of 318 points—the second highest, and the most points scored by a non-kicking player in Penn State's history.

"Saquon is head and shoulders above what a normal athlete should do in this day and age," Penn State running back coach Charles Huff told a reporter.

Barkley received many awards and honors during his college career. He received the Big Ten's Offensive Player of the Year, and the Paul Hornung Award given to the athlete chosen as the nation's most versatile player. He was also the first player ever to be named Big Ten running back of the year, returner of the year and offensive player of the year in the same season. But Barkley's time at Penn State wasn't only about football. He got good grades, performed community service projects, and served on the Lion's Leadership Council.

On March 24, 2018, the Pennsylvania townships of Coplay and Whitehall held "Saquon Barkley Day," with a parade and other events in his honor. An estimated 5,000 people attended. Barkley signed autographs and posed for pictures with fans. Politician Jeanne McNeall, a member of the Pennsylvania House of Representatives, told a reporter she proposed the celebration to honor Barkley "not because he is a famous sports star, but rather because he is an exemplary role model—honest, kind, and respectful. Saquon gives people a reason to smile."

Hear the Lion Roar

After three impressive football seasons at Penn State, Barkley felt the time was right to declare himself eligible for the NFL draft. He had proven himself to be one of the best college football players in the United States. There was only one place to go from here, and that was the NFL.

Barkley was moving to the Giants, but said he would never forget Penn State. "It has been an honor and a privilege to call Penn State home. I will continue to work each and every day to continue to represent Penn State the right way as I move on to the next phase of my life," he announced on social media.

NY Giants Coach Pat Shurmur believes Barkley is the strong running back the Giants need to bring new life to the team.

Going Home

ONE OF THE THINGS NFL teams look for in new players is their overall athletic ability. Coaches want to know that a player is athletic outside of his chosen sport. To give scouts and recruiters a chance to look at players doing a variety of athletic activities, the NFL holds a Combine. Barkley participated in the 2018 Combine held in Indianapolis on March 2. He amazed recruiters by running a 40-yard dash in 4.4 seconds. He also jumped 41 inches and bench pressed 225 pounds for 29 repetitions. At the NFL Combine, draftees also interview with coaches and general managers to see if they will be a good fit for a team.

Barkley's performance at the Combine cemented his position as a top pick at the NFL draft. It also showed the Giants officials that Barkley would be strong on their team.

Barkley answers questions from the media during the NFL Scouting Combine on March 1, 2018.

On July 22, 2018, Barkley signed a contract with the New York Giants. He would play for New York for four years. In return, he would earn $31.2 million.

The Giants had high expectations for Barkley. The prior season had been a disaster for the team. Out of 16 games, the Giants had won only three. It was the most losses in one season in team history. Coach Shurmur believed a strong running back was needed to bring new life to the team, and he said he was sure that Barkley was the man to accomplish this. Barkley was fast as he zig-zagged across the field. He was hard to tackle. He was 6 feet tall and weighed 233 pounds, and he charged right through players who tried to block him. He jumped over human hurdles. Any opposing team member who tried to stop him simply seemed to bounce off him. He rushed, received, blocked. And sometimes he did all three in the same game.

"He does everything," Charley Casserly, a former Washington Redskins and Houston Texans general manager told a reporter for the *New York Times*. "Home-run ability with speed, ability to run inside with quickness. He's got some power to him, can change directions. He can catch the ball really well—much better than most running backs—and can do it spread out in the formation."

Barkley played his first game as a Giant on September 9, 2018, against the Jacksonville Jaguars. He rushed for 106 yards and made 1 touchdown. Still, the Giants lost 20-15. In his first 10 season games as a Giant, Barkley scored 7 touchdowns. In a game against the Tampa Bay Buccaneers, he scored 2 touchdowns.

Barkley is learning that playing for the NFL is different than playing high school or even college football. For one thing, there's a different playbook to learn. He also has to face a different defense each week.

"There is always room for improvement on anything. I am seeing the field a lot differently. [I am learning] where I have to be in my pass concepts," he told the Associated Press in June 2018.

"[W]e know what we expect from him. He's also a rookie, and there's certain things that you have to do. The good news is, he understands what he has to do and he's doing it," Coach Shurmur told the *New York Times*. Only time will tell if Barkley will perform the miracles that the Giants need. As for Barkley, he believes he is in the right place at the right time. He had hoped the Giants would draft him because he was born in New York, and he feels like he has come home.

"This is where I wanted to end up. Being able to play for the New York Giants [is] amazing and truly an honor," he told a reporter.

Barkley soars over Adrian Amos of the Chicago Bears at MetLife Stadium in New Jersey on December 2, 2018. He rushed for 125 yards during the game.

CHAPTER FIVE

A Giant of a Man

GETTING DRAFTED by the New York Giants wasn't the only exciting thing to happen to Barkley in April 2018. Two days before the draft, he became a father. His girlfriend, Anna Congdon, gave birth to their daughter Jada Clare on April 24.

"I pray that I can be the best father to you and help you grow into an amazing woman," Barkley shared his happiness with his daughter on social media.

Family has always been important to Barkley. "My family is not perfect and has been through a lot," he says. "But the stuff they went through is the reason I am who I am today, he told a reporter.

Barkley has learned a lot from his parents. One of the things they have taught him is to be kind to others. He is generous with his time, especially with his fans. When he played for Penn State, he would spend hours signing posters after the games. Once, in an airport, Barkley gave fans his cleats when they asked him for a picture. Another time he gave cleats to an NFL prospect before the Combine, after Barkley learned the young man was working out in Timberland boots. And when he was still in high school, Barkley gave a gold medal that he had won for a 100-meter dash to a runner who had to rerun the race—and lost after winning the first time.

"It felt really good to do a good deed and put a smile on her face. I think I learned it from my mom and my family. It was the right thing to do," Barkley told a reporter.

His fans are important to Barkley and he enjoys meeting and spending time with them, proving once again he is a giant of a man.

Barkley runs the ball against the Chicago Bears at MetLife Stadium on December 2, 2018. The Giants won the game 30-27.

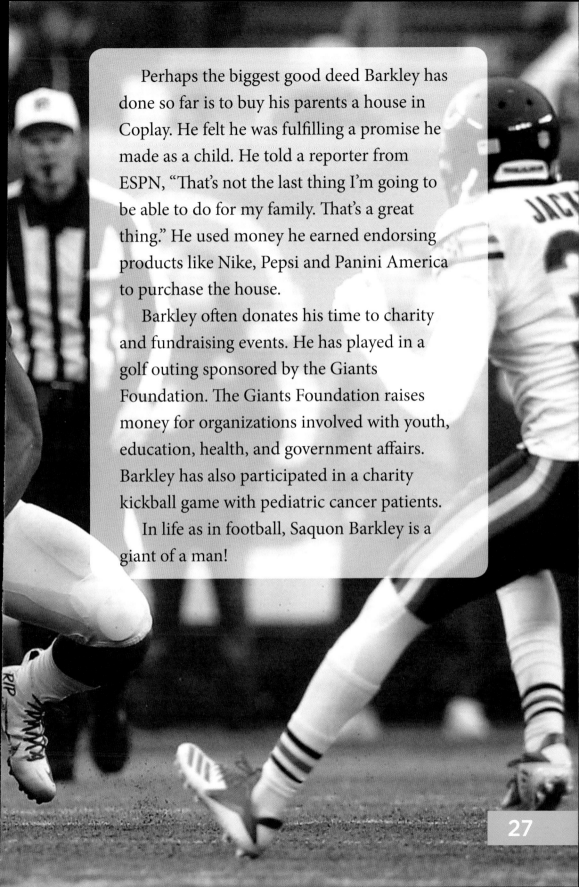

Perhaps the biggest good deed Barkley has done so far is to buy his parents a house in Coplay. He felt he was fulfilling a promise he made as a child. He told a reporter from ESPN, "That's not the last thing I'm going to be able to do for my family. That's a great thing." He used money he earned endorsing products like Nike, Pepsi and Panini America to purchase the house.

Barkley often donates his time to charity and fundraising events. He has played in a golf outing sponsored by the Giants Foundation. The Giants Foundation raises money for organizations involved with youth, education, health, and government affairs. Barkley has also participated in a charity kickball game with pediatric cancer patients.

In life as in football, Saquon Barkley is a giant of a man!

Timeline

1997   **Born February 7**

2013   **Commits to Rutgers University during junior year in high school**

2014   **Changes his mind about Rutgers and commits to Penn State**

2016   **Wins two Big Ten Offensive Player of the Week awards**

2017   **- Receives several Big Ten Offensive Player of the Week awards**
            - Receives Graham-George Big Ten Offensive Player of the Year
            - Wins Ameche-Dayne Big Ten Running Back of the Year and
              2017 Rodgers-Dwight Big Ten Return Specialist of the Year
            - Leaves Penn State to go professional and enter the NFL draft

2018   **- Participates in NFL Combine**
            - Drafted by the NY Giants
            – Plays first game as a NY Giant against Jacksonville Jaguars

Quick Stats 2014-2018

Total carries	244
Total rushing yards	1,198
Total rushing touchdowns	10
Average yards per carry	4.9

Find Out More

Web sites

Documentary about Saquon Barkley
Saquon Barkley: The Making of a Superstar. His Story, His Family
https://www.youtube.com/watch?v=bPQgTQI8PoM

Giants Select RB Saquon Barkley
https://www.youtube.com/watch?v=c5ntRydIQr8

NY Giants website
https://www.giants.com/

NFL website
https://www.nfl.com/

Rules of NFL Draft
https://operations.nfl.com/the-players/the-nfl-draft/the-rules-of-the-draft/iants

Books

Bradshaw, Chris. *New York Giants Football Quiz: 50 Questions on Big Blue.* CreateSpace Independent Publishing Platform, 2018.

Cohen, Robert W. *The 50 Greatest Players in New York Giants History.* Lyons Press: Guilford, CT, 2018.

Editors of Sports Illustrated. *1st and 10 (Revised and Updated): Top 10 Lists of Everything in Football (Sports Illustrated Kids Top 10 Lists).* Sports Illustrated Kids, 2016.

Gramling, Gary. *The Football Fanbook: Everything You Need to Become a Gridiron Know-it-All (A Sports Illustrated Kids Book).* Sports Illustrated Kids, 2017.

Jacobs, Gregg. *The Everything Kids' Football Book: All-time Greats, Legendary Teams, and Today's Favorite Players—with Tips on Playing Like a Pro.* Adams Media, 2016.

Works Consulted

Associated Press. "Saquon Barkley learning about being an NFL running back." *USA Today*. June 12, 2018. https://www.usatoday.com/story/sports/nfl/2018/06/13/saquon-barkley-learning- about-being-an-nfl-running-back/36005941/

Baskin, Ben. Face of the NFL? "Saquon Barkley Has a Plan." *Sports Illustrated*. April 18, 2018. https://www.si.com/nfl/2018/04/18/saquon-barkley-2018-nfl-draft

"Penn State's Saquon Barkley ranked the No. 32 player in the nation by Pro Football Focus." *Penn Live*. 29 June 2016 https://www.pennlive.com/pennstatefootball/index.ssf/2016/06/penn_states_saquon_barkley_ran_1.html

Martinelli, Michelle R., "7 superhuman Saquon Barkley moments from his final season at Penn State." *USA TODAY*, Jan. 2, 2018. https://ftw.usatoday.com/2018/01/saquon-barkley-penn-state-football-highlights-best-plays-moments-2017-nfl-draft

Newsmaker Q&A: Whitehall High senior Saquon Barkley, gave away gold medal. *The Morning Call*, May 16, 2015. https://www.mcall.com/news/local/mc-newsmaker-saquon-barkley-20150516-story.html

Pickel, Greg. "Saquon Barkley named Big Ten offensive player, return specialist and running back of the year." 1 Dec. 2017. *Penn Live*. https://www.pennlive.com/pennstatefootball/index.ssf/2017/11/saquon_barkley_named_big_ten_r.html

Ramirez, Edgar. "Saquon Barkley becomes a father, awaits turning pro all in one week," *Pittsburg Post Gazette*. April 25, 2018. https://www.post-gazette.com/sports/psu/2018/04/25/Saquon-Barkley-baby-daughter-Jada-Clare-Barkley-Anna-Congdon-Instagram-NFL-Draft/stories/20180425014.

"Saquon Barkley gets the call from Pat Shurmur." Youtube. http://www.nfl.com/videos/nfl-draft/0ap3000000929073/Barkley-gets-the-call-from-Shurmur-I-promise-I-won-t-let-you-guys-down

Schonbrun, Zach. "Saquon Barkley and the Impossible Hype Machine." *The New York Times*. August 8, 2018. https://www.nytimes.com/2018/08/08/sports/saquon-barkley-giants.html

Thamel, Pete. "A Lion in Summer." *Sports Illustrated*, vol. 126, no. 3, July 2017, pp. 92-97. EBSCOhost, search.ebscohost.com/login.aspx?direct=true&db=fth&AN=124224624&site=ehost-live.

Wogenrich, Mark, "Born to Run: Saquon Barkley's journey from the Bronx to Pennsylvania to Penn State to Pasadena" *The Morning Call*. December 17. 2016. https://www.mcall.com/sports/college/psu/mc-penn-state-football-saquon-barkley-father-20161217-story.html

"In Coplay 5000 turn out for Saquon Barkley Day" March 24, 2018. https://www.dailypress.com/mc-spt-saquon-barkley-coplay-parade-20180321-story.html)

Saquon Barkley on the Giants: "This is where I wanted to end up." *The Morning Call*. April 28, 2018. https://www.mcall.com/sports/college/psu/mc-spt-saquon-barkley-new-york-giants-20180427-story.html

Index

About the Author

Marylou Morano Kjelle is a college English professor and freelance writer who lives and works in Central New Jersey. Marylou has written nearly 60 nonfiction books for young people of all ages. Her sports biographies include Derrick Rose, Tim Howard, Josh Wolfe, and Alex Rodriquez. Marylou enjoyed writing about Saquon Barkley, who plays for one of the two New Jersey "home football teams." She loved learning even more about football by writing this book.